The Dolls in the House At the Top of the Hill

THE EXTRAORDINARY ANTIQUE DOLL COLLECTION OF JUNE ELLEN LANE

Theriault's
the dollmasters

To order additional copies contact:
Dollmasters, PO Box 2319, Annapolis, MD 21404
Tel. 800-966-3655   Fax 410-571-9605
www.dollmasters.com

Design: Travis Hammond
Photography: Gerald Nelson
Production Design: Cindy Gonzalez
Senior Conservator: Terry Lanford

$69
ISBN: 1-931503-69-9
Printed in Hong Kong

This antique doll collection auctioned by Theriault's

of Annapolis, Maryland, January 7-8, 2011.

www.theriaults.com.

The Dolls in the House At the Top of the Hill

There are so many beautiful dolls in this book from the collection of the late June Ellen Lane of Lake Arrowhead, California. But this is not the first time that the dolls have taken center stage. For the collectors of southern California and for attendees at UFDC national conventions, the dolls will be familiar friends. Because this generous woman believed in sharing. The door of her home "at the top of the hill" in Lake Arrowhead was always open to eager and inquisitive doll collectors, researchers, and, of course, the doll club members of the Bébés of the Woods doll club she helped form. And her dolls travelled to many national and regional UFDC conventions which is the reason that, today, so many bear the blue ribbon award that they, justifiably and proudly, earned.

The nature of the June Ellen Lane collection, encompassing hundreds and hundreds of the world's rarest dolls, is difficult to pinpoint. A piqued curiosity, an aching knowledge to learn more about a particular category of dolls, a historical connection, or simply "I fell in love with her face" were what inspired June Ellen Lane to choose her items. The choices were sometimes intellectual and sometimes purely emotional and sometimes whimsical. At a past Theriault auction, June Ellen bid and won a grand 60" British pedal car, and when Stuart Holbrook queried her, "June Ellen, why did you buy that? That seems so out of your collecting sphere," she just replied, "Well, it was made during my birth year, so I thought it should be in my home". It was the same notion that explained her love for a large Dora Petzold doll, also to be offered at the auction; as she explained in a 1998 feature article about her collection in the

Mountain News, "the doll was made in 1925, the year I was born, and also the face is so wonderful and has such an expression".

"Her ideology of collecting was never to settle on just any doll or any type of doll. She would collect the rare example made for that particular type of doll," notes Stephanie Patterson, friend and fellow collector, adding "She was a true master at doll collecting." Her collection of dolls by Jules Steiner is an example. Patterson related that June Ellen wanted the complete series of Steiner dolls ("she was desperately on the hunt for the missing alphabet") but would never compromise on beauty or quality.

She was fascinated by early fashion ladies, from the English and Continental wooden dolls of the 18th century to the splendid French bisque poupées of the mid-19th century. In looking at a panorama of these dolls from her collection – and, yes, it is a veritable panorama – it is clear that not only beauty of face and rarity of model informed her choices, but also a rarity or innovation in body style. A fellow collector clarified this, "Beauty did not have to be a pretty doll, it could also be uniqueness or other rare qualities." Happily, beauty and rarity usually combined in the Lane collection, and in that regard, collectors will find in this book not only wonderful fully-articulated wooden bodies, but also those models whose design was so unique as to demand a brevete from the French court. There is the rare model by Benoit Martin, a Leverd & Cie poupée with distinctive deposed body style, a Dehors lady with unique body as well as neck articulation, Petit & Dumoutier wooden-bodied lady with pewter hands, a wooden-bodied mystery lady with metal joints, several hollow-leather bodies by Clement, and more. Stephanie Patterson noted, "Often she would leave the fashion dolls undressed, displaying the total beauty of the doll. She would often insist that I should explore different types of dolls. 'Branch out' she would say."

It may have been this same fascination with the dollmaker's quest to create a body that perfectly combined artistic qualities with functionality that drew her attention to the extremely rare French automaton "Charmeuse de Serpent" by Roullet & Decamps when it came for auction. After all, the automaton maker needed to create a spectacular and dramatic presentation, but one that would still allow agile movement of the six elaborate animations that the Snake Charmer performed. Or maybe June Ellen Lane just simply loved the piece. At any rate, it stood center-stage in her home, just inside the entrance, and now will be center-stage at the January event.

A conversation between Stuart Holbrook and June Ellen Lane before the auction of "Charmeuse de Serpent" says something about the robust character and will of this sweet and sharing lady. When June Ellen called to say she was interested in bidding on the piece, Stuart cautioned her that two very competitive and eager bidders, men collectors, from Europe were registered to bid for that very same item. Her comment? "Stuart, I will show those European men what a determined California woman can do when her mind is set." And she did.

June Ellen Lane's stalwart and resilient character was clothed in a sharing and sensitive personality. It may have been her life story. A Chicago native, a child of the Depression era, she made her way to

California just after World War II, and remained there for her lifetime. Yet she never forgot her roots. One of her last purchases was a complete set of "Women of History" dolls from an exhibition that had been commissioned for the 1939 Chicago World's Fair which she attended as a child.

It could be said that June Ellen Lane was the American dream; from humble origins to a beautiful home and life well-lived in her dream home at Lake Arrowhead. Surrounded by the dolls that she loved, she embodied the American pioneer spirit.

As for the title of this book. It was chosen from a story told by one of her doll collector friends, who stopped to ask directions to her house. The neighbor responded, "Oh, you're looking for the lady who lives with the dolls in the house at the top of the hill". June Ellen Lane would be pleased to be remembered that way. ❋

Session 1

Friday, January 7, 2011

At the Westin South Coast Plaza

Newport Beach, California

Preview 6 PM · Auction 7 PM

2. German All-Bisque Doll in Original Costume with Presentation Box

4" (10 cm.) One-piece all-bisque head and torso, brown glass eyes, painted features, closed mouth, blonde mohair wig, pin-jointed bisque arms and legs, painted white stockings with blue rims, black one-strap shoes. Condition: generally excellent. Comments: Germany, circa 1895. Value Points: pristine condition, the little doll wears original white plush coat with cord and bead ties, matching cap, undergarments, and is presented in a richly-decorated card paper box with a fabric-trimmed lithograph on its cover depicting a little girl in winter garb. $400/600

3. Precious German Bisque Closed Mouth Child by Kestner in Petite Size

9" (23 cm.) Bisque socket head, brown glass inset eyes, painted lashes, dark eyeliner, brush-stroked and feathered brows, accented nostrils and eye corners, closed mouth with very full lips, accent line between the lips, blonde mohair wig, early composition and wooden fully-jointed body with straight wrists, wearing antique royal blue silk dress with ivory silk trim, undergarments, stockings, leather shoes signed 1/0 and a superb woven high-peak bonnet with blue silk banding and lining. Condition: generally excellent. Marks: 11. Comments: Kestner, circa 1884. Value Points: most endearing petite size with fine quality of sculpted features, beautiful painting, original body, fine antique costume. $1100/1500

1. Wonderful German Bisque Closed Mouth Doll known as "A.T. Kestner"

21" (53 cm.) Bisque socket head with very full cheeks and angular pointy-tip nose, blue glass sleep eyes, dark eyeliner, painted dark curly lashes, rose-blushed eye shadow, brush-stroked and multi-feathered brows, accented eye corners and nostrils, closed mouth with defined space between the shaded and outlined lips, blonde mohair wig over plaster pate, early composition and wooden fully-jointed body with straight wrists, wearing antique sailor costume, undergarments, stockings, black leather shoes, grand sailor cap. Condition: generally excellent. Marks: 14. Comments: Kestner, circa 1885, the model is known as the "A.T. Kestner" for its resemblance to the French A.T. bébé of the same era, whose market the doll attempted to capture. Value Points: a rare large size of the desirable and rarely-found model, with lovely bisque having a delicate luminous patina, superb sculpting with "first-from-the-mold" definition, wonderful antique costume. The doll was acquired by June Ellen Lane from a previous Theriault's auction, "Cotillion" and was featured for several years on a Theriault shopping bag, stationery and other ephemera. $6000/8500

4. Stunningly Beautiful Early German Bisque Doll Attributed to Simon and Halbig

19" (48 cm.) Pale bisque socket head with oval-shaped face, almond-shaped blue glass enamel inset eyes, delicately-curled painted lashes, dark eyeliner, shaded feathered brows, accented nostrils and eye corners, closed mouth with defined space between the outlined shaded lips, pierced ears, blonde mohair wig, Sonnenberg composition and wooden fully-jointed body with straight wrists. Condition: generally excellent. Marks: 5. Comments: attributed to Simon and Halbig, circa 1885, the model closely resembles their 905 child model. Value Points: exceptionally beautiful early closed-mouth doll with compelling intent expression, finest quality of bisque and painting, original body and body finish, superb antique brocade and silk satin dress and matching bonnet, undergarments, stockings, leather shoes. $4000/5500

5. Superb French Bisque Poupée by Leontine Rohmer with Bisque Hands and Feet

19" (48 cm.) Pale bisque swivel head with flat-cut neck socket on bisque shoulder plate, very plump facial features, neck articulation allowing realistic 90 degree swivel, cobalt blue glass inset eyes, thick dark eyeliner, painted lashes, feathered brows, accented nostrils, closed mouth with primly-set accented lips, unpierced ears, pale blonde lambswool wig, cork pate, softly-stuffed Rohmer kid poupée body with pull-strings in torso for sitting, kid over-wooden upper arms, ball-jointed knees, bisque lower arms and legs with individually sculpted or defined fingers and toes. Condition: generally excellent, professional repair to right middle finger. Marks: (Rohmer stamp on torso). Comments: Leontine Rohmer, circa 1860, the poupée evidences distinctive brevete features of Rohmer, including the realistic neck articulation and body style. Value Points: superb model of the rare early bisque poupée with wonderful facial expression enhanced by very deeply modeled features, very fine original body with bisque limbs, and wearing fine original costume comprising black velvet fitted jacket with bead trim, black taffeta skirt, and matching bonnet, with watch and fob. The doll has a blue ribbon award from 1995 UFDC national convention. $6000/8500

6. Very Rare and All-Original Early Bisque Child

10" (25 cm.) Pale bisque swivel head with flat-cut neck socket allowing realistic 90 degree articulation, bisque shoulder plate, brilliant cobalt blue glass tiny eyes, delicately-painted lashes and brows, accented nostrils, closed mouth with center accent line, un-pierced ears, blonde mohair wig, kid body with shapely torso, bisque lower hands, bisque lower legs with bare feet. Condition: generally excellent. Comments: maker unknown, circa 1865. Value Points: superb doll with exquisite facial expression, very rare neck articulation in the Rohmer manner, original body with bare feet, and wearing her original wonderful cut-work and embroidered dress. $3500/4500

7. Very Beautiful Petite French Bisque Portrait Poupée by Eugene Barrois

15" (38 cm.) Pale bisque shoulder head with very slender oval face and elongated throat with defined hollow, cobalt blue glass inset eyes, heavy eyelids, dark eyeliner, painted curly lashes, delicately feathered brows, accented eye corners and nostrils of elegantly curved nose, closed mouth with slightly-upturned lips corners suggesting an enigmatic smile, pierced ears, brunette mohair wig over cork pate, very firm kid poupée body with shapely torso, legs and ankles, bisque arms from above the elbows with sculpted fingers. Condition: generally excellent. Marks: E. 2 Depose B (low on front shoulder plate). Comments: Eugene Constant Barrois, circa 1865, the portrait model closely resembles the beloved Empress Eugenie of France. Value Points: exceptionally beautiful poupée with very refined and elegant features, finest quality of bisque and painting, wonderful original kid body with bisque arms and exquisitely-sculpted hands, superb gown of cream gauze with interwoven silk ribbons, blue silk flower garlands in her hair, turquoise jewelry. $6500/8500

8. Fine French Hat and Leather Purse for Poupée

To fit 16"-17" poupée. The hat, of tightly woven cord bands has a flat brim and is decorated with bronze silk ribbons and banding, along with a spray of white and purple/black tiny berries and leaves; with original muslin lining. Along with a tan kidskin purse with accordion sides and silver clasp. Excellent condition. French, circa 1865. $300/500

9. French Bone-Handled Parasol

9" (23 cm.) Having a carved bone handle, the parasol is covered with original (frail) blue silk and decorated with blue and cream silk fringe. French, circa 1865. $300/500

generally excellent. Comments: for the French market, circa 1890. Value Points: the beautiful swivel-head doll wears her original silk and lace dress with silk ribbon trim, undergarments and purse, and is presented in an early fancy box with accessories that are still tied to gilt and paper-edged cards, including silk cape and hankies, along with bone-handled brush, comb, puff, and paper-wrapped soap and sachet. $600/1100

12. An All-Original Pair of German Bisque Dolls in Elaborate Chinese Costumes

10" (25 cm.) Each has bisque socket head, dark glass eyes, painted lashes and brows, closed mouth, five-piece paper mache body. Condition: generally excellent. Marks: 13/0. Comments: German, circa 1890, probably for the French market. Value Points: wonderfully-preserved pair, wearing their original elaborate costumes, the girl in rose silk kimono with double bands of embroidery at the edges, over silk trousers and slippers, and with gilt metal ornament on her tasseled head-dress, tassel ties, and carrying a basket of silk flowers in an

10. French Bisque Bébé by Rabery and Delphieu in Superb Original Original Presentation Box

12" (30 cm.) Bisque socket head, amber brown glass paperweight inset eyes with spiral threading, dark eyeliner, painted curly lashes, rose-blushed eye shadow, brush-stroked and multi-feathered brows, shaded nostrils, closed mouth with outlined shaded lips, upturned lip corners, pierced ears, blonde mohair wig over cork pate, French composition and wooden eight-loose-ball-jointed body with straight wrists. Condition: generally excellent. Marks: R 4/0 D. Comments: Rabery and Delphieu, circa 1884. Value points: in pristine unplayed with condition, having beautiful complexion and bisque, the brown-eyed bébé has early original body and is presented in the base of the original presentation box which is edged with paper lace and red silk ribbons; the box contains an assortment of original couturier costumes: maroon silk dress, maroon velvet tall bonnet with plumes and silk ribbons, maroon woolen sailor-style dress, rose sateen jacket, and a white pique ensemble with exquisite handwork comprising taufling wrap, jacket, cap and bib. The bébé wears her original crisp muslin chemise and woolen knitted booties. A French newspaper, dated 1885, is laid in the box. The doll was a blue ribbon winner in the 1999 UFDC national convention. $7500/9500

11. French All-Bisque Mignonette in Presentation Box with Trousseau

4 ½" (11 cm.) Bisque swivel head on bisque torso, cobalt blue glass enamel eyes, painted features, closed mouth, blonde mohair wig, peg-jointed bisque arms and legs, painted white stockings with blue rims, black two-strap shoes. Condition:

11.

embroidered silk basket; the boy in a simple ivory and blue silk costume over brown silk trousers, and with stacked heels, black cap over a very long queue. $1100/1500

13. Very Beautiful French Bisque Bébé by Leon Casimir Bru, Size 4

15" (38 cm.) Bisque swivel head on kid-edged bisque shoulder plate with modeled bosom and shoulder blades, almond-shaped blue glass paperweight inset eyes with spiral threading and dark iris rims, dark eyeliner, dark painted curly lashes, rose-blushed eye shadow, brush-stroked and multi-feathered brows, accented nostrils, closed mouth with defined tiny tongue tip between the outlined lips, pierced ears, brunette human hair over cork pate, French kid bébé body with kid-over-wooden upper arms, bisque forearms, Chevrot-hinged hips, wooden lower legs. Condition: generally excellent. Marks: Bru Jne 4 (head) No 4 Bru Jne (shoulders). Comments: Leon Casimir Bru, circa 1885. Value Points: superb example from the golden age of Bru with entrancing eyes, very pronounced exquisite modeling, beautiful bisque and painting, original body, perfect bisque hands, and wearing a lovely antique costume comprising navy blue dress, white cotton pinafore with scalloped-edge embroidery, knit stockings, old French black leather shoes. $13,000/18,000

14. Rare French Bisque Poupée with Kid-over-Wooden Body and Alice Couterier Label

15" (38 cm.) Bisque swivel head on kid-edged bisque shoulder plate, almond-shaped blue glass enamel inset eyes, delicately-painted eyeliner and lashes, feathered brows, accented nostrils and eye corners, closed mouth with center accent line, pierced ears, blonde mohair wig over cork pate, kid-over-wooden body with unusual "baggy leg" construction at the dowel-jointed knees, bisque arms from above the elbows with separately-sculpted bisque fingers, beautifully-costumed in peach silk with cream and navy blue trims. Condition: generally excellent. Marks: Maison Alice Couterier Paris 8 Rue Dauphin (original paper label). Comments: Marie Emmanuel Cruchet deposed the body model in 1862 (see Theimer, *The Panorama of Parisienne Dolls*, pp 215-217); the body style appeared with various facial models but was made for a few years only; this example was commissioned for Aux Enfants de France, the doll shop of Alice Couterier, circa 1865. Value Points: rare model with well-preserved deposed body, beautiful bisque face and perfect hands, original wig, original shop label. $4000/6000

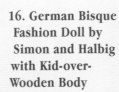

15. Charming and Petite German Bisque Doll with Painted Eyes

10" (25 cm.) Solid domed bisque shoulder head with very plump face, painted yellow pate, painted facial features, brilliant cobalt blue eyes in slightly side-glancing pose, painted red and black upper eyeliner, lightly-feathered brows, accented nostrils, closed mouth with center accent line, blonde lambswool wig, muslin stitch-jointed body with porcelain hands. Condition: generally excellent. Comments: Germany, circa 1885, attributed to Alt, Beck and Gottschalk, circa 1880. Value Points: most endearing petite early doll with beautifully-painted features. $800/1000

16. German Bisque Fashion Doll by Simon and Halbig with Kid-over-Wooden Body

10" (25 cm.) Pale bisque swivel head on kid-edged bisque shoulder plate, cobalt blue glass inset eyes, dark eyeliner, delicately-painted lashes and brows, accented nostrils, closed mouth with accent line between the primly-set lips, un-pierced ears, brunette mohair wig, stretched-kid-over-wooden body with articulation at shoulders, elbows, hips and knees, bisque

hands, wearing (frail) antique silk gown, undergarments, nice old brown leather shoes. Condition: generally excellent, finger repair on left hand. Comments: Simon and Halbig, circa 1880. Value Points: rare early model with fully-articulated kid-over-wooden body, beautiful face enhanced by contrasting brilliant eyes and pale bisque. $1100/1500

17. German Black-Complexioned Porcelain Doll in Trunk

3" (8 cm.) One-piece porcelain figure of young child, standing with arms outstretched and hands clasped, has rich black complexion and is costumed in red and grey flannel suit. The doll is presented in an early paper-covered wooden trunk with mirror on the inside, along with a paper listing the original owners of the doll. Germany, mid-19th century. $200/400

18. Extremely Rare German Bisque Lady with Bisque Tam and Matching Boots by C.F. Kling

13" (33 cm.) Bisque shoulder head portraying an adult lady with oval-shaped face and elongated throat, sculpted ash-blonde hair arranged in long flowing curls that tumble onto her shoulders and are waved across her forehead, topped by an exuberant green and white plaid tam with magenta stripes, rose and black checkered border and tri-color plumes, and having blue glass inset eyes with dark eyeliner, painted lashes and brows, accented nostrils and eye corners, closed mouth with center accent line, fully-sculpted pierced ears, and sculpted bodice with gilt-edged collar and polka-dotted blue scarf, original muslin stitch-jointed body with bisque lower arms, painted bisque ankle boots in plaid design with painted laces, antique gown. Condition: generally excellent. Mark: 5 D (in script)3. Comments: C.F. Kling, circa 1870. Value Points: extremely rare and beautiful model of which few are known to exist, its rarity points include fabulously decorated bisque tam with matching boots, sculpted bodice, glass eyes, and original body. The doll has blue ribbon awards from two UFDC national conventions. June Ellen Lane acquired the doll from the Margaret Hartshorn collection. $8000/11,000

18 detail.

18 detail.

20 detail.

19. Very Beautiful French Bisque Portrait Poupée by Jumeau

19" (48 cm.) Bisque swivel head on kid-edged bisque shoulder plate, almond-shaped cobalt blue glass enamel eyes, dark eyeliner, painted lashes, mauve-blushed eye shadow, feathered brows, accented nostrils and eye corners, closed mouth with outlined lips, pierced ears, blonde mohair wig over cork pate, kid poupée body with gusset-jointing at hips, knees and elbows, stitched and separated fingers. Condition: generally excellent. Comments: Pierre-Francois Jumeau, circa 1875, the luxury poupée model referred to as "portrait" for its distinctive presence. Value Points: wonderfully-preserved poupée with very sturdy original body, original wig in elaborate coiffure, superb bisque and painting, antique sheer muslin gown, undergarments, jewelry, leather ankle boots. $4000/5500

20. Tiny French Bisque Poupée by Jumeau, Size 00, with Original Costume, Parasol and "J" Shoes

10" (25 cm.) Bisque swivel head on kid-edged bisque shoulder plate, large pale blue glass enamel inset eyes, dark eyeliner, feathered brows, accented nostrils and eye corners, closed mouth with center accent line, pierced ears, blonde mohair wig over cork pate, French kid poupée body with stitched and separated fingers. Condition: generally excellent. Marks: 00. Comments: attributed to Jumeau, circa 1875. Value Points: very rare tiny size 00 poupée with beautiful bisque, entrancing large eyes, very sturdy original body, original mohair wig in

21 detail.

21 detail.

hip-length braids, and wearing her original costume, chemise, stockings, leather ankle boots impressed "J" and "00", matching pressed flannel bonnet, jewelry, and carrying bone-handled parasol with silk fringe. $3500/4500

21. Superb German Lady with Elaborately-Sculpted Cafe-au-Lait Hair and Ornaments

20" (51 cm.) Bisque shoulder head portraying an adult lady with heart-shaped face, elongated slender throat, cafe-au-lait sculpted hair waved across her crown, then combed loosely backward to be captured in a snood, with one well-detailed ringlet curl on either side of her throat, painted blue eyes in well-defined eye sockets, red and black upper eyeliner, single-stroke brown brows, aquiline nose with accented nostrils, closed mouth with center accent line, pierced ears,

muslin stitch-jointed body with bisque lower arms and legs, highly-defined sculpting of fingers, painted boots and tassels. Condition: generally excellent. little chip at tip of left thumb, left leg reglued. Comments: Germany, circa 1865, attributed to Conta and Bohme. Value Points: superbly-beautiful doll whose rarity factors include cafe-au-lait hair color, gilt sculpted bow at her crown, deeply-sculpted snood with lustre-trimmed tassels, exceptional detail of sculpting of facial features and fingers, and wonderful early blue silk costume with silk tassel fringe, jewelry, floral bouquet, blue velvet faux-dance card on gilt metal chatelaine. $3000/4500

French Dolls by Theimer, page 459. Value Points: very rare model with lovely presence, brown eyes rare for poupées, original wig, superb antique costume, undergarments, jewelry, shoes signed C.M. and jewelry. The doll has a blue ribbon award from 2008 UFDC convention. $4000/6000

22. Rare French Bisque Poupée with Petit & Dumoutier Lady Body and Fine Early Costume

17" (43 cm.) Bisque socket head, brown glass enamel inset eyes, delicately-painted lashes and brows, rose-blushed eye shadow, accented eye corners, closed mouth, outlined pale lips, pierced ears, brunette mohair wig over cork pate, French wooden lady body with shapely torso, loose-ball-jointing at shoulders, elbows, hips and knees, jointed wrists, metal hands. Condition: generally excellent. Marks: 4 (head). Comments: Petit & Dumoutier, circa 1877, the distinctive body was used for their doll only, with metal hands; the body is shown in *The Encyclopedia of*

23. Beautiful Early Poupée with Rare Brown Eyes and Dehors Articulation

16" (41 cm.) Bisque swivel head on kid-lined bisque shoulder plate, deposed articulation neck jointing that allows the head to tllt side to side and forwards as well as the traditional swivel, brown glass enamel inset eyes, eyeliner, painted lashes, feathered brows, accented nostrils and eye corners, closed mouth with outlined lips, ears pierced into the head, original blonde mohair wig over cork pate, kid poupée body with shapely torso, gusset-jointing at elbows, hips and knees, stitched and separated fingers, original muslin chemise, pantalets, stockings, along with antique lavender silk gown trimmed with Alencon lace. Condition: generally excellent, body especially clean and sturdy. Comments: circa 1870, the doll has the articulated neck system deposed by Dehors in 1866 which allows the head to be moved in a realistic fashion rather than just rigidly side to side. Value Points: very beautiful poupée with rare brown eyes, rare head articulation system, beautiful fresh body, lovely bisque and painting. $2800/3500

24. Gorgeous French Bisque Bébé E.J. by Jumeau, Size 11

24" (61 cm.) Bisque socket head, large amber brown glass paperweight inset eyes with spiral threading, thick dark eyeliner, lushly-painted lashes, mauve-blushed eyeshadow, arched feathered brows, accented eye corners, shaded nostrils, closed mouth with defined space between the shaded and outlined lips, separately-modeled pierced ears, blonde mohair wig over cork pate, French composition and wooden fully-jointed body with straight wrists. Condition: generally excellent. Marks: Depose E 11 J (head) Jumeau Medaille d'Or Paris (body). Comments: Emile Jumeau, circa 1885. Value Points: exceptionally beautiful model whose crisp sculpting seems as though "first-from-the-mold", dramatic large eyes, finest bisque and painting, original body, body finish, wig, and wearing very fine early embroidered cut-work dress with matching ruffled bonnet, embroidered undergarments, and cream kidskin shoes stamped "Au Bébé Bon Marche, Simonet, 63 Rue de Sevres". $7500/9000

25. Superb Early Wooden Lady with Carved Hair and Documented Costume

22" (56 cm.) One-piece carved wooden head and shapely torso with defined bosom and tiny waist, depicting an adult lady with oval-shaped face and elongated throat, sculpted brown hair with deeply-defined combmarks, in center-parted style waved away from her face into a rolled chignon at the back of her head, inset enamel dark eyes with heavy eyelids, painted brows, aquiline nose, closed mouth, pierced ears, dowel-jointing at shoulders, elbows, hips and knees, sculpted bare feet, original blue paint on torso and upper limbs. Condition: generally excellent. Comments: mid/late-18th century, a highly-refined variation of the classic Santos figure, probably southern France. Value Points: exceptionally beautiful lady doll with rare enamel eyes for this model, fully-sculpted lady body, her superb antique costume was designed and created by the London-based renowned London stage designer David Walker, at the request of her previous owner, John Darcy Noble, While in the care of Mr. Noble, the doll was named Madame, and she resided in a special niche overlooking his dining table. $12,000/15,000

26. Extremely Rare and Early 18th Century Wooden Doll with Carved Stomacher

17" (43 cm.) Carved wooden head with solid dome, flat-cut neck socket that pivots on torso dowel, well-defined features with carved eye sockets, closed mouth sculpted as open though, painted facial features, black pate under original tacked-on wig, sculpted ears, highly-defined torso with modeled bosom, sculpted definition of chemise with sculpted stomacher form, dowel-jointing at shoulders, elbows, hips, and knees, well-defined hands and feet. Condition: structurally excellent, the original finish is extremely worn and re-painted, wig is original but very worn. Comments: Continental, early 18th century. Value Points: very rare early doll with sculpted stomacher form. The doll has a blue ribbon award from 1993 UFDC national convention. $2500/3500

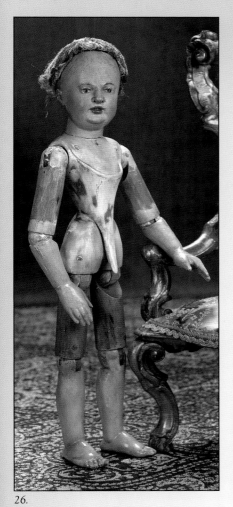

26.

27. Superb Early Continental Wooden Doll, Probably Augsburg, 18th Century

27" (69 cm.) One-piece carved wooden head and shapely torso, ivory-painted complexion over gesso undercoat, deeply-defined sculpting of eye sockets with heavy upper eyelids, painted brown eyes, single-stroke brows, aquiline nose, closed mouth with well-defined lips, blushed cheeks and chin tip, original blonde flaxen wig in elaborate original coiffure, dowel-jointing at shoulders, elbows, hips and knees, pin-jointed wrists, separately-carved fingers, original glued-on black leather slippers with buckles, wearing early black velvet and silk costume and undergarments with handmade lace. Condition: generally excellent. Wooden hands may be retouched, facial complexion original with possible early touch-up on nose. Comments: Continental, probably Augsburg, 18th century. Value Points: rare early doll with exquisite detail or original coiffure, wonderful sculpting details including double chin, beautiful eyes, original well-preserved fully-articulated body. A nearly identical doll is shown in *Children's Toys of Yesteryears, Studio Magazine*, May, 1932, page 20. The doll was acquired by June Ellen Lane from the auction of the Winter Haven Museum of Dolls and Toys in March 1985, and also has an award ribbon from the 6th annual exhibition of UFDC in Boston, 1955. $8000/13,000

27 detail.

29. French Bisque Poupée by Maison Huret with Extensive Trousseau and Trunk

17" (43 cm.) Bisque swivel head on kid-edged bisque shoulder plate, plump facial modeling, blue glass enamel inset eyes with spiral threading, dark eyeliner, painted lashes, feathered brows, accented nostrils and eye corners, closed mouth with accented lips, pierced ears, blonde mohair wig over cork pate, all-wooden fully-articulated body with shapely torso, dowel-jointing at shoulders, elbows, wrists, hips and knees, pivot jointing at upper legs. Condition: generally excellent. Marks: Medaille d'Argent Huret 22 Boulevard Montmartre Paris Exposition Universelle 1867 (green stamp on front torso). Comments: Maison Huret, circa 1868. Value Points: a lovely poupée with grand eyes and expressive features, fine bisque, fully-articulated wooden body allowing for infinite posing, is contained in an early French poupée trunk with original maker's label, along with an extensive trousseau comprising three early gowns in the "mode enfantine" style, capes, jacket, various undergarments and nightwear, linen pinafore, three bonnets, two pairs of shoes, two parasols, jewelry and accessories, and more. $15,000/20,000

28. French Bisque Poupée with Highly-Expressive Features, Possibly Bru

22" (56 cm.) Bisque swivel head on kid-lined bisque shoulder plate, very full lower cheeks and defined double chin, small blue glass enamel inset eyes, dark eyeliner, painted lashes, lightly-feathered brows, accented nostrils and eye corners, closed mouth with outlined lips, pierced ears, brunette mohair wig over cork pate, French kid poupée body with gusset-jointing at the hips, knees, and elbows, stitched and separated fingers, nicely costumed in patterned silk with embroidered velvet trim and lace collar, undergarments, leather shoes. Condition: generally excellent. Comments: possibly an early poupée model by Leon Casimir Bru, circa 1862. Value Points: very expressive features achieved by very full lower cheeks, defined double chin, hollows under the eyes, and slightly-upturned nose tip, and with fine quality bisque and painting. $3500/4500

30. French Bisque Character, 237, by SFBJ with Flocked Hair

16" (41 cm.) Solid domed bisque socket head with flocked brown hair, blue glass inset eyes in half-moon shape, painted brown curly lashes, incised eyeliner, brown brush-stroked brows, accented nostrils, slightly-parted outlined lips, row of porcelain teeth, French composition toddler body with jointing at shoulders and hips, wonderfully costumed in brown velvet Sunday best ensemble. Condition: generally excellent. Marks: SFBJ 237 Paris 6. Comments: SFBJ, circa 1912. Value Points: especially fine quality of modeling especially around the eyes, enhanced by fine lustrous patina of complexion. $2500/3500

31. French Bisque Glass-eyed Character, 238, by SFBJ

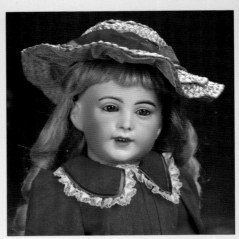

14" (36 cm.) Bisque socket head, small blue glass enamel inset eyes, curly brown lashes, brush-stroked and feathered brows, accented nostrils and eye corners, slightly-parted lips, row of little porcelain teeth, blonde human hair wig with ringlet curls, French composition and wooden fully-jointed body, nicely dressed in red silk in the antique style, undergarments, saddle shoes, antique woven bonnet. Condition: generally excellent, body wear and retouch on legs. Marks: SFBJ 238 Paris 4. Comments: SFBJ, circa 1912. Value Points: a hard-to-find model from the SFBJ 200 character series with very pleasing expression and bisque. $1100/1500

32. French Bisque Character, 235, by SFBJ

16" (41 cm.) Solid domed bisque socket head with sculpted boyish hair, defined forelock, brown glass inset eyes, painted brown curly lashes, incised eyeliner, one-stroke brows, accented nostrils, closed mouth with smiling expression, two upper beaded teeth, shaded lips, French composition and wooden fully-jointed body, well-costumed in linen romper suit with red cord trim, brown tan ankle boots with cord ties. Condition: generally excellent. Marks: SFBJ 235 Paris 6. Comments: SFBJ, circa 1912. Value Points: fine detail of sculpting especially of dimples and laugh creases around the mouth and eyes. $1100/1500

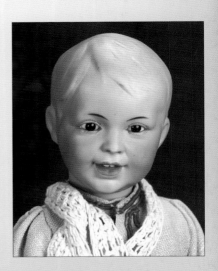

33. Two German Bisque Miniature Dolls in Amusing Antique Costumes

5" (13 cm.) and 6 ½". Each has bisque head, sculpted short blonde curly hair, painted blue eyes, red and black upper eyeliner, single-stroke brows, accented nostrils of rounded nose, closed mouth, jointed arms and legs. Condition: generally excellent, some tiny chips at stringing holes. Comments: Germany, circa 1890. Value Points: whimsical handmade costumes of big and little brothers playing knights in armor, the armor being simply silver cloth, each with little carved wooden sword. $300/500

33.1. Cotton Print Dropped-Waist Dress and Woven Bonnet with Plaid Ribbons

To fit child doll about 18"-20", 4" shoulder width. Of vibrant red and burguny print with black lattice frame, the dress features a fitted yoke above blouson bodice, gathered skirt, wide puffed sleeves with fitted cuffs, and black velvet ribbon trim, with lined bodice. Along with a black tightly-woven bonnet with graduated width brim, red silk twill lining, and decorated with Scottish plaid silk ribbon, lace and silk flowers. Excellent condition. Circa 1890. $500/700

34. Beautiful French Bisque Bébé by Gaultier with Early Block Letter Signature

21" (53 cm.) Bisque socket head with very plump cheeks, amber brown glass paperweight inset eyes, thick dark eyeliner, painted lashes, arched feathered brows, accented nostrils and eye corners, closed mouth with defined space between the outlined lips, pierced ears, brunette human hair wig over cork pate, French composition and wooden eight-loose-ball-jointed body with straight wrists, beautifully dressed in red silk frock with fine lace trim, ruffled lace bonnet, undergarments, knit stockings, black leather shoes signed with full figure of a doll. Condition: generally excellent. Marks: F. 9 G. Comments: Gaultier, circa 1880, their earliest period bébé. Value Points: especially fine depth of modeling enhanced by rich decoration of features, original early body and body finish, superb costume. $4000/5500

35.

35. German Porcelain Lady Doll with Ornately-Sculpted Black Hair

19" (48 cm.) Porcelain shoulder head of adult lady with slender face and elongated throat, black sculpted hair drawn away from face and formed into rolled curls at the sides, and then gathered into an elaborate arrangement of curls at her neck that tumble onto her back shoulders and are clasped by a beaded hair ornament, painted bright cobalt blue eyes, red and black upper eyeliner, single-stroke brows, accented nostrils, closed mouth with slightly upturned lip corners, old muslin stitch-jointed body with leather arms, sewn-on red muslin stockings, black kid boots, wearing beautiful antique blue taffeta dress with black silk fringe, undergarments. Condition: generally excellent. Comments: Germany, circa 1870. Value Points: rare model with beautifully-detailed feathering of hair at the sides of her forehead, brilliant large eyes. $900/1400

37.

36. German Porcelain Lady Doll with Elaborately Up-swept Coiffure

22" (56 cm.) Porcelain shoulder head of adult lady with slender oval face and elongated throat, black sculpted hair artfully drawn away from her face and decorated at the crown with an ornamental comb, with looped curls forming a coronet and extending into arranged curls at the back with a single long curl onto her nape, painted pale blue eyes, red and black upper eyeliner, one-stroke brows, closed mouth, sculpted pierced ears, early commercial kid body, nicely costumed in burgundy taffeta with black velvet and lace trim. Condition: generally excellent. Comments: Germany, circa 1870. Value Points: the very rare coiffure is enhanced by decorative comb, artistic feathering detail of hair around the forehead edge. $1500/1800

37 detail.

37. Rare German Porcelain Lady Doll with Very Elaborate Coiffure

18" (46 cm.) Lightly-tinted porcelain shoulder head of adult lady with heart-shaped face, very elongated throat, black sculpted hair waved away from her face, captured by a sculpted hair band, and enhanced with artistically-painted stippling all-around the forehead; a long ringlet curl behind each ear falls to the front or side of her

36.

shoulders and the back of her hair is pulled up and captured in an elaborate bouquet of ringlet curls that tumble one on top of the other; with delicately-painted facial features including shaded blue eyes, red and black upper eyeliner, single-stroke brows, aquiline nose with accent dots, closed mouth with extended center accent line, early muslin stitch-jointed body with porcelain lower limbs, painted flat black shoes, wearing early transfer-print cotton gown with ribbon trim, and undergarments. Condition: generally excellent. Comments: Germany, circa 1850, Value Points: extremely rare model with superbly sculpted hair and ears, beautiful painting of features and complexion. The doll has two blue ribbon awards from UFDC conventions, and was acquired by June Ellen Lane from the Margaret Hartshorn collection. $2500/3500

38. Very Rare German Porcelain Lady with Wigged Slit Head

17" (43 cm.) Richly pink-tinted porcelain shoulder head depicting an adult lady, slender oval face and elongated throat, slightly-modeled bosom, un-tinted and un-glazed solid dome with cut slit at the crown for wig placement, heavily molded eyelids with red and black upper eyeliner, single-stroke brows, accented nostrils, closed mouth with center accent line, early braided human hair wig, all-leather antique body with stitch-jointing and stitched and separated fingers, wearing changeable-silk taffeta gown, undergarments, leather shoes, bonnet. Condition: generally excellent. Comments: Germany, circa 1870. Value Points: rare slit dome construction for wig placement, very beautiful sculpting of features with rich complexion and patina. June Ellen Lane acquired the doll from the Margaret Hartshorn collection. $1500/2500

39. Very Beautiful Large German Porcelain Lady with Modeled Bosom and Rare Coiffure

26" (66 cm.) Pink-tinted porcelain shoulder head of adult lady with oval-shaped face and elongated throat, modeled bosom, black sculpted hair combed smoothly over her head and looped back to form into a tight

39.

chignon of five braided coils, painted blue upper glancing eyes, red and black upper eyeliner, single stroke black brows, beautifully-shaped nose with accented nostrils, closed mouth with defined lips, old muslin stitch-jointed body, pink-tinted porcelain arms from above the elbows with beautifully-sculpted hands. Condition: generally excellent. Marks: (illegible numbers inside the head). Comments: Germany, circa 1850. Value Points: rare early model in wonderful large size, with beautiful complexion, rare coiffure, molded bosom, rare matching hands with superb detail, and wearing wonderful dotted muslin white gown with layered undergarments, green kid slippers. $4000/5500

40. Large French Bisque Poupée by Alexandre Dehors with Lovely Smiling Expression

24" (61 cm.) Pale bisque swivel head on kid-edged bisque shoulder plate, with extra neck articulation allowing the head to modestly nod forward and flirtatiously tilt side to side, brilliant cobalt blue glass enamel inset eyes, dark eyeliner, painted lashes, arched feathered brows, accented nostrils and eye corners, closed mouth with slightly upturned lips in enigmatic smile, ears pierced into the head, blonde mohair wig over cork pate, kid poupée body with gusset-jointing at hips and knees, stitched and separated fingers and toes, pretty antique dress, undergarments, stockings, shoes, bonnet, jewelry. Condition: generally excellent. Comments: Alexander Dehors, circa 1867, who deposed the head articulation system to allow more realistic posing of the doll. Value Points: rare early model is enhanced by most beautiful facial expression, fine quality of bisque and painting. $3200/4000

41. Beautiful French Bisque Poupée Attributed to Dehors

15" (38 cm.) Pale bisque swivel head on kid-edged bisque shoulder plate, almond-shaped blue glass enamel inset eyes, dark eyeliner, painted lashes, feathered brows, accented nostrils and eye corners, closed mouth with outlined lips, pierced ears, blonde mohair wig over cork pate, French kid poupée body with gusset-jointing at hips, knees, and elbows, stitched and

separated fingers, costumed in the 1868 French style in fine navy blue and maroons silks with matching bonnet, undergarments, shoes, stockings. Condition: generally excellent. Comments: attributed to Dehors who, in 1867, registered his system for allowing the doll to tilt her head side to side, or to nod, as well as swivel. Value Points: superb artistry of the facial modeling and painting, very sturdy and clean original kid body, extra-articulations of head allowing realistic and pleasing poses. $3000/4000

42. French 19th-Century Accessories for Large Poupée or Bébé

16"l. parasol. Comprising a rose silk parasol with wooden handle and cut-crystal hand-grip; corsage in original cardboard cone holder with silk flowers, lace and rose silk streamers and bow; and a pair of woven finger-less gloves with wrist ruffle and defined thumb opening. Excellent condition. French, circa 1875, suitable for accessorizing large poupée or bébé. $400/600

43. French Silk Parasol for Poupée, and Bonnet

8" (20 cm.) l. parasol. Comprising a brass-handled parasol with bone hand-grip and tip, bone tips at each tine, textured ivory silk cover with ivory braid edging and ivory silk fringe; along with a wire-framed bonnet with twill cord cover and decorated with a coronet of tiny white, blue and rose flowers, with aqua silk streamers. Very good condition, chip to bone tip of parasol, bonet a tad dusty. French, circa 1865, the parasol has superb luxury details of materials and construction. $300/600

44. Superb French Bisque Wooden-Bodied Poupée from Au Paradis des Enfants

18" (46 cm.) Pale bisque swivel head with flat-cut neck socket on bisque shoulder plate with swivel-locking construction allowing the head to pivot only in a realistic 90 degrees, brilliant cobalt blue enamel inset eyes in narrow eye sockets, dark eyeliner, painted lashes, feathered arched brows, accented nostrils and eye corners, closed mouth with outlined lips, un-pierced ears, blonde wig over original kid cap and cork pate, stretched-kid-over-wood fashion body with shapely torso, dowel-jointed shoulders, elbows, hips and knees, bisque forearms with sculpted fingers, elongated thighs. Condition: generally excellent. Marks: F 4 G (block letters on front rim of shoulder plate) Au Paradis des Enfants, Perreau Fils 156 Rue Rivoli, 1 Rue du Louvre (stamp on torso). Comments: the poupée was commissioned from Gaultier by the prestigious Parisian toy store, Au Paradis des Enfants, circa 1867; the store presented only the most luxurious dolls and playthings to its society clientele. Value Points: beautiful early poupée with rare body style, rare deposed swivel head mechanism, choicest bisque, perfect bisque hands, original shop label and wearing a superb antique day dress with demi-train and lace trim. $4000/6500

Comments: Emile Jumeau, earliest period of the EJ model, circa 1882, the C remains an elusive marking but may refer to Carrier-Belleuse who is known to have sculpted the Bébé Triste for Jumeau during this period. Value Points: rare and sought-after model is seldom found, this example with very beautiful bisque and painting, original signed body with original finish. $6000/8500

46. French 19th-Century Maple Wood Doll Chair

13" (33 cm.) The maple wood chair with bamboo-style carvings has its original (very frail) tufted seat cushion, and its fine original finish. Excellent condition except seat. French, circa 1885. $400/600

47. Three 19th-Century French Jewelry Boxes with Paris Scenes

3 ½" (9 cm.) square, the largest. Each has gilded metal or ormolu frame with richly embossed or beaded ornamentation, and hinged lid that opens to reveal a tufted red or blue silk cushion. The largest has beveled glass sides, another has gilded metal sides, and the third has glass sides with faux-marble finish. The beveled glass lid of each box encloses a tinted scene of Paris, two of Tour Eiffel at its time of construction, and the third being an early color engraving with heightened varnish at the windows. Two square boxes are excellent, triangular has some wear. French, mid/late 19th century. $400/600

48. Petite French Bisque Poupée Attributed to Alexandre Dehors

12" (30 cm.) Bisque swivel head on kid-edged bisque shoulder plate, with deposed head articulation allowing the doll to nod and tilt head side to side as well as swivel, cobalt blue glass eyes, narrow eye sockets, black eyeliner, feathered brows, accented nostrils, closed mouth with accented lips, ears pierced directly into head, blonde mohair wig over cork pate, kid poupée body with shapely torso, gusset-jointing at hips and knees, kid-over-wooden upper arms, bisque forearms. Condition: generally excellent. Marks: 0.

45. Rare and Sought-After Early Period French Bisque EJ Bébé by Jumeau

18" (46 cm.) Bisque socket head with plump lower cheeks, large gray glass spiral-threaded eyes with darker grey iris outer-rims, painted lashes, pronounced mauve eye shadow, brush-stroked brows, accented nostrils and eye corners, closed mouth with defined space between the shaded and outlined lips, separately-applied pierced ears, blonde mohair wig over cork pate, French composition and wooden eight-loose-ball-jointed body with straight wrists, old costume is included. Condition: generally excellent. Marks: C EJ (head) Jumeau Medaille d'Or Paris (body).

Comments: attributed to Alexandre Dehors, circa 1867, who deposed the charming head articulation with this description, "These new movements make available to the dolls either a modest sense of superiority, as if to say, 'Go ahead, Huret doll, see if you can do the same' or a more aggressive sense of superiority, along the lines of a firmly declared 'Don't you dare, I'm patented'." Value Points: charming petite size with beautiful bisque hands and face, rare neck articulation, original antique costume that pleasingly complements her cobalt blue eyes. $2500/3500

49. Very Beautiful French Bisque Bébé by Schmitt et Fils with Signed Body

14" (36 cm.) Bisque socket head with transitional facial model, blue glass spiral-threaded inset eyes with dark eye iris rims, dark eyeliner, delicately-painted lashes, mauve-blushed eye shadow, brush-stroked brows, accented nostrils and eye corners, closed mouth with defined space between the pale outlined lips, pierced ears, lambswool wig over cork pate, French composition and wooden eight-loose-ball-jointed body with flat-cut derriere, lovely old costume, jewelry, undergarments, black kidskin shoes signed "P" in script and "0", antique woven bonnet. Condition: generally excellent. Marks: Sch (in shield on head and derriere) 0 (head). Comments: Schmitt et Fils, circa 1882, the facial model is a transitional from round-face to pear-shaped face. Value Points: especially beautiful model with splendid eyes, original signed body, lovely bisque, the doll was featured on the cover of *Doll Classics* by Jan Foulke. $10,000/15,000

50. Two German All-Bisque Bathing Beauties

6" (15 cm.) reclining. Each is one-piece all-bisque figure of adult nude lady, each with sculpted short brown curly hair, painted facial features, one posed half-reclining on her back with bent knees, one foot extended, one arm modestly held to her face (her right hand is restored); the other is seated, slightly leaning forward with hands in expressive pose. Condition: excellent except as noted above. Comments: Germany, circa 1915. Value Points: superb detail of sculpting and expression. $600/900

51. German Porcelain Lady Doll from Bavarian Arts and Crafts Series

15" (38 cm.) Porcelain shoulder head of adult lady with sculpted oval face and elongated throat, sculpted light brown hair, heavily-lidded downcast eyes, painted brows, aquiline nose with accent dots, closed mouth, defined throat hollow, muslin stitch-jointed body, porcelain lower arms with expressive fingers, painted shoe ribbons, wearing antique silk gown. Condition: generally excellent, one finger tip chipped. Comments: from the series of artistic porcelain dolls presented at the Bavarian Arts and Crafts Institute, early 20th century, inspired by famous master sculptures or paintings of the Renaissance era. Value Points: superb artistry both in sculpture and painting of features and complexion on the rare doll. $1700/2500

52. German All-Bisque Bathing Beauty in Rare Large Size

17" (43 cm.) One-piece all-bisque figure of adult lady posed with head tilted backward, right elbow bent and posed behind her head, feet elegantly posed with painted white ballet slippers, painted facial features include blue upper glancing eyes, red and black upper eyeliner, rose blushed eye shadow and cheeks, closed mouth in smiling expression with a row of painted teeth, brunette mohair wig. The bisque figure is nude with frail remains of her factory-original silk undergarment. Condition: restoration to both hands, one thumb and two fingers missing. Comments: Germany, circa 1910. Value Points: very rare large size with beautifully-sculpted details. $500/700

51.

52.

53. Two Large German Porcelain Bathing Beauties, One with Dressel & Kister Signature

10" (25 cm.) reclining. Each is one-piece all-porcelain with sculpted hair and painted facial features, one reclining on her side, with bent knees and elbows, her head resting on her left palm, and the other in a seated pose, a red hair band wrapped around the loosely coiled hair, her hands clasping her left ankle. Condition: restoration on ankles and feet of seated lady; excellent condition of reclining lady. Marks: (Dressel and Kister blue stamp on reclining lady). Comments: circa 1910. Value Points: rare larger size in scarce porcelain medium, one with maker's signature. $600/900

54. Large German All-Bisque Nude with Sculpted Gold Hair Band

13" (33 cm.) One-piece all-bisque figure of nude lady designed to be posed standing upright or reclining on her side, having both arms extended, feet posed on toes (with original holes in feet for posing upright) and having sculpted smoke-grey hair pulled into a fashionable chignon with painted gold wide hair band decorated with little red beads, painted brown eyes, black eyeliner, thick brown brows, neck haughtily tilted upward.
Condition: generally excellent. Comments: Germany, circa 1910. Value Points: rare model with exquisite detail of sculpting in fine larger size. $500/800

55. Rare German Porcelain Lady Doll with Highly-Characterized Features Known as Nymphenburg Lady

13" (33 cm.) Solid domed porcelain shoulder head of adult lady with very angular face leaning to the right, elongated throat, modeled bosom, heavily-lidded painted grey eyes, black upper eyeliner, single-stroke brows, aquiline nose, closed mouth, brunette mohair wig, French kid poupée body. Condition: generally excellent. Comments: possibly one of the models created by the Bavarian Association of Arts and Crafts in the early 20th century; the dolls were inspired by historical sculptures and paintings and were produced in very limited numbers in Nymphenburg at Koniglich Bayerische Porzellan-Manufaktur. Value Points: rare model with superb sculpted features and painting, fine antique body with very fine early rose silk costume. $1500/2200

Marks: Paris 7. Comments: Henri Delcroix, circa 1888. Value Points: bébés by this firm are extremely rare to find, this example with very expressive wide-eyed face enhanced by lovely painting, original body and body finish, lovely costume. $7500/9500

57. German Bisque Lady with Modeled Bosom

11" (28 cm.) Bisque shoulder head of adult lady with head tilted to the side, elongated throat and modeled bosom and cleavage, painted blue upper glancing eyes, red eyeliner, single-stroke brows, padded armature body, bisque forearms with expressively-posed fingers, antique costume of grey velvet and bronze silk. Condition: generally excellent. Comments: Germany, circa 1900. Value Points: rare-to-find model with original bisque hands, lovely painting of features. $300/500

58. French Bisque Poupée with Brown Eyes Attributed to Doleac & Cie, Size 0

12" (30 cm.) Bisque swivel head on kid-edged bisque shoulder plate, brown glass enamel inset eyes, dark eyeliner, painted dark lashes, feathered brows, accented nostrils and eye corners, closed mouth with center accent line, pierced ears, kid poupée body with gusset-jointing at hips, knees and elbows, stitched and separated fingers, beautifully costumed in the antique style in rich silks and satins, undergarments, leather slippers. Condition: generally excellent. Marks: 0. Comments: attributed to Louis Doleac & Cie, circa 1867. Value Points: charming petite size 0, lovely bisque and painting, very sturdy original body. $2800/3500

59. Very Beautiful French Bisque Bébé EJ, Size 1, by Jumeau with Gilt-Signed Jumeau Shoes

8 ½" (22 cm.) Bisque socket head, blue glass paperweight inset eyes, dark eyeliner, lushly-painted lashes, brush-stroked brows, accented nostrils, closed mouth with outlined lips, pierced ears, blonde mohair wig over cork pate, French composition and wooden fully-jointed body with straight wrists, nicely costumed in silk dress with lace trim, bonnet, original Jumeau petticoat and pantalets, socks, shoes. Condition: generally excellent. Marks: Depose E. 1 J. (head) Jumeau Medaille d'Or Paris (body). Comments: Emile Jumeau, circa 1884. Value Points: rare petite size with beautiful hip-length mohair wig, choice bisque, dramatic eyes, original

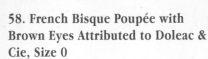

56. Very Rare French Bisque Bébé with Dramatic Eyes by Henri Delcroix

18" (46 cm.) Bisque socket head, very large blue glass paperweight inset eyes, lushly-painted dark lashes, rose-blushed eye shadow, brush-stroked and feathered brows, accented nostrils of elegantly-shaped nose with pointy-tip, closed mouth with defined space between the outlined lips, dimpled chin, pierced ears, blonde-mohair wig over cork pate, French composition and wooden fully-jointed body, wearing antique green velvet and silk dress, undergarments, leather boots signed with imprint of full figure of a doll, straw woven bonnet. Condition: generally excellent.

body and body finish, original Jumeau socks and black kidskin Jumeau shoes with brown silk rosettes, signed in gilt letters "Bébé Jumeau Med d'or Paris Depose" and incised "1". $7500/9500

60. Blue-Eyed French Bisque Bébé Triste by Emile Jumeau, Size 13 with Nadaud Store Label

28" (71 cm.) Bisque socket head, deep blue glass paperweight inset eyes, thick dark eyeliner, painted lashes, mauve-blushed eye shadow, brush-stroked and multi-feathered brows, accented eye corners, shaded nostrils, closed mouth with defined space between the outlined shaded lips, dimpled chin and philtrum, separately modeled pierced ears, original blonde mohair wig over cork pate, French composition and wooden fully-jointed body with plump limbs, straight wrists, wearing antique blue silk jester costume with matching jester cap and party rattle. Condition: generally excellent. Marks: 13 (head) Nadaud 34 rue de 4 septembre Paris (paper label on body). Comments: Emile Jumeau, circa 1884, the bébé was presented at the Paris toy store of Jeanne Nadaud, notable for its prestige dolls. Value Points: excellent modeling with deeply-defined features, the bébé has the sought-after gentle expression desired on this model, and very lovely bisque, original wig, pate, body, body finish, and rare store label. $14,000/18,000

61. French Bisque Bébé by Jumeau with Mulatto Complexion, Original Costume

13" (33 cm.) Bisque socket head with golden brown (mulatto) complexion, amber-brown glass paperweight inset eyes, dark eyeliner, dark painted lashes, black brush-stroked brows, accented nostrils and eye corners, open mouth, accented lips, row of sculpted teeth, black fleecy wig over cork pate, French brown-complexion composition and wooden fully-jointed body, wearing cotton suit, straw bonnet and necklace of gold coins. Condition: generally excellent. Marks: 4. Comments: Emile Jumeau, circa 1895. Value Points: especially beautiful complexion with fine lustrous patina, original body and body finish, original costume. $1800/2500

62. French Bisque Bleuette in Trunk with Costumes

12" (29 cm.) Bisque socket head, blue glass sleep eyes, painted lower lashes, feathered brows, open mouth, row of teeth, brunette human hair wig, French composition and wooden fully-jointed body. Condition: generally excellent. Marks: 71 Unis France 149 301 1 ¼. (head) 2 (body) 1 (feet). Comments: Bleuette, circa 1935. Value Points: the doll is presented with a red Bleuette trunk along with a variety of original costumes including Coupe Davis 1962, Sans Facon 1951, Valisere with original label, Bien-Etre 1952, Mosaique 1955, Robe Standard 1948, several accessories, and two additional recent costumes in the Bleuette style. $1200/1500

63. French Bisque Character Toddler, 251, by SFBJ

13" (33 cm.) Bisque socket head, blue glass sleep eyes, mohair lashes, painted curly lashes, painted lower lashes, short feathered brows, accented nostrils, open mouth,

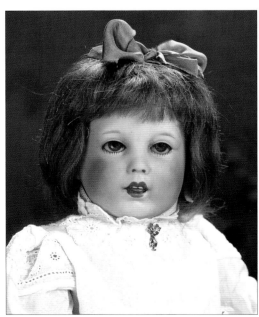

shaded and accented lips, two porcelain upper teeth, tongue, brunette mohair bobbed wig, French composition and wooden fully-jointed toddler body, nicely costumed. Condition: generally excellent. Marks: SFBJ 251 Paris 4 (head) (SFBJ paper label on torso). Comments: SFBJ, circa 1915. Value Points: very expressive features, original wig and lashes, original signed body. $1100/1500

64. Pair, French Terra Cotta Character Dolls "Yerri" and "Gretel" in Original Costumes and Boxes

9" (23 cm.) Each is all terra cotta with socket head, painted hair, large blue painted side-glancing googly eyes, painted long upper lashes, button-shaped nose, closed mouth with little pursed lips and extended laughing lip line, five-piece terra cotta body, painted shoes and socks. Condition: very good, original finish with some typical minor wear. Marks: Paris (head). Comments; designed by the French artist, Hansi and distributed by J.P. Gallais & Cie, the dolls were created in 1917 to celebrate the return of Alsace to French control; the dolls were presented at the Concours des Poupées in Paris in 1917 and received a First Prize. Value Points: wearing the original costumes of Alsatian boy and girl, including original Alsatian coiffe with French flag emblem, each carries a cardboard slateboard with their name and "Vive la France". The boy Yerri carries a French flag, while Gretel carries a parasol, and each is presented in its original box with printed illustration of the doll by Hansi on the lid. $800/1000

65. French Bisque Glass-eyed Character, 227, by SFBJ in Original Box

16" (41 cm.) Solid domed bisque socket head, brown sculpted and painted hair with forelock detail, brown inset eyes in small half-moon eye sockets, brown curly lashes, single-stroke brows, accented nostrils, very slightly-parted lips in cheerful smiling expression, row of porcelain upper teeth, French composition and wooden fully-jointed body, wearing original blue and white checkered uniform and undergarments, stocks, shoes. Condition: generally excellent. Marks: SFBJ 227 Paris 6. Comments: SFBJ, circa 1912, from their art character series. Value Points: very fine detail of sculpting especially laughter lines around the eyes and mouth, fine quality of bisque, presented in original box with label "Le Bébé a Tete Caractere". $2000/3000

67. Wonderful All-Original German Bisque Toddler by Kammer and Reinhardt

10" (25 cm.) Bisque socket head, blue glass sleep eyes, mohair lashes, brush-stroked and feathered brows, accented nostrils, open mouth, two porcelain upper teeth, brunette mohair bobbed wig, composition toddler body with jointing at shoulders and hips, starfish-shaped chubby fingers, hip-jointing. Condition: generally excellent. Marks: K*R Simon & Halbig 126 Germany 23. Comments: Kammer and Reinhardt, circa 1917. Value Points: impeccable original condition, with wonderful-eyed expression, rosy cheeks, original wig, original body and body finish, and wearing elaborate original folklore costume, hat and shoes. $800/1000

68. Very Dear German Bisque Character, 251, by Marseille

10" (25 cm.) Bisque socket head, tiny blue glass sleep eyes, short painted lashes and brows, rounded nose with painted nostrils, slightly-parted lips, two porcelain upper teeth, brunette mohair wig in long braids, composition and wooden ball-jointed toddler body with side-hip jointing. Condition: generally excellent. Marks: 251 G.B. Germany A 7/0 M DRGM 248/1. Comments: Marseille, for George Borgfeldt, circa 1920, the model was commissioned from Marseille for the important American doll importer, George Borgfeldt under a special registration; Borgfeldt enlisted many American artists in the design of his dolls and it is likely that this is such an example although the designer's name remains unknown at this time. Value Points: all-original doll with highly-characterized features, lovely bisque, original wig, body, body finish and costume. $600/900

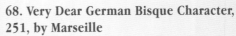

66. An All-Original German Bisque Child in Folklore Costume by Heinrich Handwerck

17" (43 cm.) Bisque socket head, blue glass sleep eyes, mohair lashes, painted lower lashes, short feathered brows, accented nostrils, open mouth, four porcelain teeth, pierced ears, blonde mohair wig, composition and wooden ball-jointed body. Condition: generally excellent. Marks: W Heinrich Handwerck Simon & Halbig Germany 0 ½ (head) Heinrich Handwerck 0 ½ (torso). Comments: Handwerck, circa 1900. Value Points: fine unplayed with condition, original wig, lashes, body, body finish, and wearing superb folklore costume with elaborate vibrant detail, gold bead earrings, original coiffe, undergarments, shoes and stockings. $800/1000

69. Rare German Bisque Child, 905, by Simon and Halbig with Closed Mouth

11" (28 cm.) Solid domed bisque socket head, pale blue glass inset eyes with darker blue outer rims, painted lashes, dark eyeliner, short feathered brows, accented nostrils and eye corners, closed mouth with outlined lips, pierced ears, pale blonde mohair wig in side-coiled braids, Sonneberg composition and wooden fully-jointed body with straight wrists. Condition: generally excellent. Marks: SH 3 905. Comments: Simon and Halbig, circa 1885. Value Points: rare model in most appealing petite size, with beautiful wide-eyed expression, lovely bisque, original body, body finish, wig, and wearing antique folklore costume with beautiful matching lace on apron and blouse. $900/1200

70. Very Rare German Bisque Doll, 1478, by Simon and Halbig with Rare Body

16" (41 cm.) Bisque socket head with slightly-elongated throat and face representing an older child, small blue glass sleep eyes, painted lashes, short feathered brows, accented nostrils and eye corners, closed mouth with accent line between the lips, pierced ears, blonde mohair wig, composition and wooden ball-jointed body with very slender and elongated torso and limbs, beautifully-shaped hands, antique Swedish folklore costume, accessories, undergarments, shoes and stockings. Condition: generally excellent. Marks: 1478 S&H 4. Comments: Simon and Halbig, circa 1900, the doll closely resembles the IV model by that same firm. Value Points: very rare model with most beautiful and expressive features, lovely bisque and sculpting, rare body style with original finish. $5000/7500

French kid poupée body with square-cut collarette, gusset-jointing at hips and knees, wooden arms and hands with dowel-jointing at shoulders, elbows and wrists, included is antique costume. Condition: generally excellent, right thumb reglued. Marks: H (head and shoulders). Comments: Leon Casimir Bru, circa 1867, from his earliest letter series poupées, the slightly-smiling model preceded his deposed smiling poupée. Value Points: rare model with lovely bisque and painting, original signed head and shoulders, original Bru body with rare wooden arms. $5000/7500

72. French Blue Silk Parasol and Woven Bonnet

12" (30 cm.) l. parasol. The painted-pale-blue wooden handle with lithographed image on the handgrip depicting angelic child, has blue silk cover and tassels with cord; along with original blue silk cover which has preserved the parasol in very fine original condition and color. Along with a two-color intricately-woven straw bonnet with a rich corsage of flowers at the crown and teal blue silk bow and streamers, muslin lining. Excellent condition. French, circa 1880. $400/700

73. Wonderful German Bisque Bunny Doll with Accessories in Decorative Presentation Box

9" (23 cm.) A bisque-headed doll with blue glass eyes, painted features, open mouth, four tiny teeth, five-piece paper mache body, is completely enclosed excepting her face in a white fur bunny costume that is decorated with

71. French Bisque Poupée, Size H, by Leon Casimir Bru with Wooden Articulated Arms

19" (48 cm.) Bisque swivel head on kid-edged bisque shoulder plate, glass enamel inset eyes with rare grey iris and violet/blue iris rim known as "tri-color" eyes, painted lashes, feathered brows, accented nostrils and eye corners, closed mouth with hint of smile, accented pale lips, ears pierced into head, original blonde mohair wig over cork pate,

delicate rose silk bows and brass bells. She is holding a tray of paper mache decorated Easter eggs, and a woven hotte basket is attached to her back contained three paper mache bunnies. The doll is presented in beautiful card paper box with rose paper cover, gilt edging, silk bows, and a color lithograph of a bunny holding a tray of eggs. Excellent condition. Germany, circa 1890, a superb presentation throughout. $1200/1600

74. Beautiful French Bisque Bébé by Leon Casimir Bru, Size 3, with Splendid Eyes

14" (36 cm.) Bisque swivel head on kid-edged bisque shoulder plate with modeled bosom and shoulder blade, very deep blue glass paperweight inset eyes, dark eyeliner, painted lashes, brush-stroked and feathered brows, accented eye corners, shaded nostrils, closed mouth with defined tongue tip between the outlined and shaded lips, pierced ears, kid bébé body with gusset-jointing at hips and knees, kid-over-wood upper arms, bisque arms with separately-sculpted fingers, nicely costumed in French style in ivory and aqua silk with lace trim, undergarments, stockings, old blue kidskin slippers. Condition: generally excellent. Marks: Bru Jne 3 (head) Bru Jne No. 3 (shoulders). Comments: Leon Casimir Bru, circa 1882. Value Points: an early period classic Bru Jne with original sturdy body, perfect bisque hands, very beautiful expression and exceptional splendid eyes. $15,000/19,000

75 detail.

75 detail.

75. French Porcelain Doll with Cobalt Blue Lever Sleep Eyes by Blampoix

20" (51 cm.) Very-lightly tinted porcelain shoulder head with plump facial shape, cobalt blue glass enamel eyes with wire-lever sleep mechanism that operates from the torso, painted all-around lashes, lightly-feathered brows, accented nostrils, closed mouth with center accent line, blonde lambs-wool wig over cork pate, kid body with shapely torso, plump legs, pink-tinted porcelain lower arms. Condition: generally excellent. Marks: B.S. (shoulder plate) (illegible green stamp on torso). Comments: Blampoix, circa 1860. Value Points: very beautiful early porcelain doll with pleasing complexion, rare sleep eyes with original mechaims, wearing wonderful antique gown with matching leggings, leading strings at the back of the gown, layered undergarments, ruffled bonnet. $4500/6500

76. French Porcelain Poupée with Cobalt Blue Glass Eyes and Fine Early Gown

17" (43 cm.) Porcelain shoulder head of adult woman with slender oval face and elongated throat, almond-shaped cobalt blue enamel glass eyes, dark eyeliner, dark painted lashes, lightly-feathered brows, accented nostrils of aquiline nose, closed mouth, accented lips, blonde mohair wig over cork pate, French pink kid poupée body with slender waist, one-piece shapely legs, one-piece arms with stitched fingers. Condition: generally excellent. Comments: French, circa 1860. Value Points: rare portrait-like model with adult features is unusual in this portrait medium, her light-tinted complexion enhanced by very dramatic eye color and eye decoration, original body, wonderful early cotton gown with pagoda sleeves, long fitted jacket, undergarments, early bonnet, red kidskin slippers. The doll has a blue ribbon award from 2002 UFDC convention. $3500/4500

77 detail.

77. German Porcelain Lady Doll with Unusual Heavily-Lidded Eyes

17" (43 cm.) Porcelain shoulder head with slender facial shape, elongated throat, black sculpted hair drawn away from her face in loose waves, with a cluster of curls at the crown and the back hair captured in a sculpted snood, deeply-sculpted eye sockets with heavy upper lids, blue upper-glancing painted eyes, red and black upper eyeliner, single-stroke brows, closed mouth with center accent line, muslin stitch-jointed body, porcelain hands and lower legs, nicely costumed in coral gown of antique silk, with antique undergarments and black velvet jacket with bead and fringe design. Condition: generally excellent. Comments: Germany, circa 1870. Value Points: superb sculpting of heavily-lidded eyes lending a dreamy expression, rare coiffure. $600/900

78. German Porcelain Doll Representing a Young Lady with Rare-To-Find Coiffure

17" (43 cm.) Porcelain shoulder head with black sculpted hair arranged in soft waves away from her face excepting the short curly forehead bangs with painted wispy tendrils, having loosely-coiled chignon at the back with a cascading curl onto her center shoulders, sculpted pierced ears, pale blue upper-glancing eyes in deeply-set eye sockets, painted thin eyeliner and brows, accented eye corners and nostrils, closed mouth, muslin stitch-jointed body, porcelain lower limbs, antique green wool/silk dress with black velvet ribbons, undergarments, matching earrings and brooch. Condition: generally excellent. Comments: Germany, circa 1875, the model aptly represents a young lady. Value Points: rare model with wonderfully-sculpted hair, her sculpted eyes set in deep sockets. $500/700

78 detail.

78 detail.

79 detail.

79. Petite German Porcelain Lady Doll with Rare Coiffure

12" (30 cm.) Porcelain shoulder head of adult lady with oval-shaped face, elongated throat, black sculpted hair waved from her face with painted wispy curls around her forehead, tightly-woven braid at the crown that extends from either side of the center part, and three ringlet curls at her nape, painted bright blue eyes, red and black upper eyeliner, accented nostrils and eye corners, closed mouth, muslin stitch-jointed body, porcelain lower limbs, painted black boots. Condition: generally excellent. Comments: Germany, circa 1870. Value Points: rare coiffure with superb details especially for petite size, antique silk gown with lace and aqua silk ribbon trim, undergarments. $500/800

80. Early German Porcelain Lady Doll with Rare Original Body and Elaborate Coiffure

24" (61 cm.) Porcelain shoulder head with very delicately-tinted complexion, oval-shaped face with slightly-elongated throat, black sculpted hair waved away from her face with stippling-details around her forehead, wide pouf curls at the sides that form into a smooth loop at each side back captured at the crown, having painted shaded-blue upper-glancing eyes, red and black upper eyeliner, single-stroke brows, circle-accents at nostrils, closed mouth with center accent line, commercial muslin stitch-jointed body, porcelain hands in slightly-cupped position with defined nails and knuckles, nicely costumed in vintage blue silk and braid, antique undergarments. Condition: generally excellent. Comments: Germany, circa 1860. Value Points: very beautiful doll with rare coiffure, refined expression, original body. $1200/1800

81. Beautiful Early German Bisque Doll with Original Folklore Costume and Provenance

20" (51 cm.) Solid domed bisque shoulder head, very pale bisque contrasting plump facial modeling, cobalt blue glass eyes, dark eyeliner, lightly-painted lashes, accented nostrils of small nose, closed mouth with outlined lips, ears pierced into her head, blushed cheeks, original commercial muslin body designed to sit or stand, bisque forearms and hands, brunette human-hair wig in hand-stitched braids. Condition: generally excellent, one thumb tip chipped. Comments: Germany, circa 1870. Value Points: very rare and beautiful early wigged model with cobalt blue eyes, original body, wearing original folklore costume, probably Danish, of velvet and wool with silk trim, undergarments, leather boots. With original frail paper note "Carry" with foreign language notes and date of Dec 18, 1870, along with her blue ribbon award from UFDC convention in 1963. $800/1200

82. German Bisque Lady Doll with Slightly-Modeled Bosom, Model 136

17" (43 cm.) Bisque swivel head on kid-lined bisque shoulder plate with slightly-modeled bosom having blushed detail, deep grey glass inset eyes with spiral threading, dark eyeliner, long painted curly lashes, rose-blushed eye shadow, feathered brows, accented nostrils and eye corners, closed mouth with defined space between the pale outlined lips, pierced ears, pink-kid pin-jointed body with bisque forearms, blonde mohair wig. Condition: generally excellent, body especially sturdy and clean. Marks: 136 6. Comments: Germany, circa 1880. Value Points: very beautiful expression with luminous eyes, lovely subtle blushing, wearing antique aqua silk faille gown, undergarments, lace cap, brown leather ankle boots. $900/1300

83. German All-Bisque Doll with Fancy Boots, Attributed to Kestner

6 ½" (17 cm.) Bisque swivel head on kid-edged bisque shoulder plate, blue glass sleep eyes, painted lashes and brows, accented nostrils and eye corners, slightly-parted lips, two upper teeth, blonde mohair wig, peg-jointed bisque arms and legs, cupped hands, shapely legs with defined knees, tiny ankles, painted white stockings with purple ties and black ankle boots with blue tassels, newer pretty cotton dress, apron and undergarments included. Condition: generally excellent, tiny typical flakes at two stringing holes.

82.

83.

Marks: 1. Comments: attributed to Kestner, circa 1885. Value Points: very dear face with bright blue eyes and plump cheeks, fancy boots. $500/800

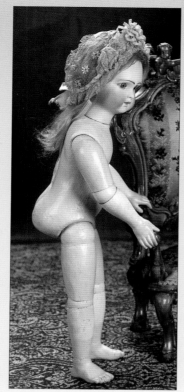

84 detail.

84 detail.

84. Very Rare Early German Doll with Original Signed Body

22" (56 cm.) Solid domed bisque head with flat-cut neck socket, two stringing holes at the top of the head, pale complexion, almond-shaped grey glass inset eyes, dark eyeliner, painted lashes and lightly-feathered brows, accented nostrils, closed mouth with defined space between the outlined lips, ears pierced into her head, blonde mohair wig, original composition and wooden eight-loose-ball-jointed body with straight wrists, protruding-dowel at upper torso that attaches to unique head neck, flat-cut derriere, newer silk costume included. Condition: generally excellent. Marks: (diamond enclosing an eight-point star which encloses an illegible symbol) Trade-Mark Schutz-Mark (marks on bottom of derriere). Comments: Germany, very early example of ball-jointed doll, circa 1880, a smaller version of this doll is shown in Cieslik's *German Doll Encyclopedia*, page 53. Value Points: very rare doll with beautiful expression and bisque, original and very rare body with maker's mark. Few examples of this doll are known to exist, and virtually never with the maker's mark. $3000/4000

85. Exquisite French Bisque Poupée by Leon Casimir Bru, Size J, Known as "Smiling Bru"

23" (58 cm.) Bisque swivel head on kid-edged bisque shoulder plate, slender elongated face, almond-shaped blue glass enamel inset eyes, dark eyeliner, painted lashes and brows, shaded nostrils, closed mouth with pale accented lips having enigmatic smiling expression, pierced ears, kid gusset-jointed body with square-cut collarette, wooden arms with dowel-jointing at shoulders, elbows and wrists, lovely silk costume. Condition: generally excellent, old retouch to arms. Marks: J. Comments: Leon Casimir Bru, circa 1872, the model is considered a portrait of the Empress Eugenie. Bru considered this facial model so significant that he took the unusual step of having the model deposed in his name. Value Points: superb modeling, bisque, and painting on the portrait poupée, in very rare larger size, with original body. June Ellen Lane acquired the doll from the Lenore Thomas collection, and it is also photographed in Mildred Seeley's book, *How to Collect French Fashions.* $10,000/14,000

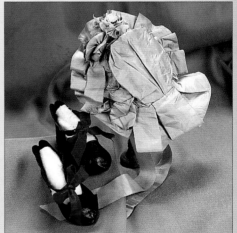

85.1. French Aqua Silk Bonnet

2 ½" (6 cm.) inside head width. Of soft aqua silk satin, the bonnet is designed to sit at the back of the head and frame the face with a wide gathered ruffle, with pleated full back and crown, bavolet neck ruffle, cream silk lining, and decorated with aqua silk ribbons and bows, and violet and cream silk flowers. French, circa 1885. Excellent condition, a beautiful and well-preserved silk fabric, the bonnet is virtually unused. $300/500

86. Very Rare French Bisque Portrait Poupée by Jumeau in Superb Antique Costume

21" (53 cm.) Bisque swivel head on kid-edged bisque shoulder plate, oval slender face, slightly-elongated throat, aquiline nose, blue enamel glass inset eyes, dark eyeliner, painted lashes, arched feathered brows, accented eye corners and nostrils, closed mouth in solemn expression with accented and shaded lips, pierced ears, brunette hand-tied human-hair wig over cork pate, kid poupée body with shapely torso, gusset-jointing at elbows, hips and knees, separately-stitched fingers. Condition: generally excellent. Marks: Jumeau Medaille d'Or Paris (body). Comments: Jumeau, circa 1878, the deluxe portrait model, likely a special commission doll, may have been exhibited at the 1878 Paris Exposition L'Universelle. Value Points: the rarity of the model is rivaled by exceptional beauty and quality of production, with original signed body, superb ivory satin gown with elongated train, undergarments, satin shoes. $8000/12,000

87. Beautiful Large French Bisque Brown-Eyed Bébé by Rabery and Delphieu

32" (81 cm.) Bisque socket head, large amber-brown glass paperweight inset eyes, thick dark eyeliner, painted dark curly lashes, rose-blushed eye shadow, widely-arched brush-stroked and feathered brows, shaded nostrils, closed mouth with shaded and outlined lips, dimpled chin and philtrum, pierced ears, brunette mohair wig over cork pate (new blonde human hair wig also included), French composition and wooden fully-jointed body, wearing wonderful antique costume comprising cut-work white cotton dress under white pique coat with more lavish embroidered cut-work, undergarments, woven bonnet, stockings, brown leather shoes with silk ribbons and silver buckles. Condition: generally excellent. Marks: R. 5 D. Comments: Rabery and Delphieu, circa 1886. Value Points: rare larger size with original body and body finish, beautiful gleaming bisque with crisp definition of features, large size examples of this bébé are rarely-found. $6000/8500

88. French Bisque Bébé by Rabery and Delphieu with Rare Double Row of Teeth

19" (48 cm.) Bisque socket head, very deep amber-brown glass paperweight inset eyes, dark eyeliner, painted lashes, rose-blushed eye shadow, brush-stroked and multi-feathered brows, accented nostrils and eye corners, open mouth with impressed dimples at lip corners. double row of tiny porcelain teeth, impressed chin dimples, pierced ears, brunette human hair wig over cork pate, French composition and wooden fully-jointed body. Condition: generally excellent. Marks: R. 1 D. Comments: Rabery and Delphieu, circa 1888. Value Points: rare model with expressive features, original body and body finish, wonderful antique costume including black leather shoes signed "Rabery Paris". $3500/4500

89. French Bisque Bébé by Rabery and Delphieu with Pretty Brown Eyes

19" (48 cm.) Bisque socket head, amber brown glass paperweight inset eyes, dark eyeliner, rose-blushed eye shadow, dark curly lashes, light-brown brush-stroked and feathered brows, accented nostrils, closed mouth with pale outlined lips, dimpled chin, pierced ears, blonde lambs-wool wig over cork pate, French composition and wooden eight-loose-ball-jointed body with straight wrists, wearing lovely antique silk plaid dress with lace bodice, matching bonnet, undergarments, old leather shoes, red knit stockings. Condition: generally excellent. Marks: R 1 D. Comments: Rabery and Delphieu, circa 1885. Value Points: very sweet bébé with luminous amber eyes enhanced by beautifully-painted eye features, original body and body finish. $3500/4800

90. Wonderful Small Doll Carriage with Romantic Dancing Ladies Garland

14" (36 cm.) Firm-sided carriage with raised designed along with carriage body depicting six Grecian-style women with flowing robes, hair and scarves in a festive dancing scene, having four spoked metal wheels, hinged canvas sunshade, porcelain hand grip, and fitted interior with removable center section so two children could seat inside, or one child could recline. Excellent condition, age and origin uncertain, designs are delightful and artistically achieved. $900/1300

91. Scottish Dollhouse Dolls in Scottish Presentation Box

3 ½" (9 cm.) A set of five dollhouse dolls with flat-dimensional drawn faces, wrapped armature bodies designed to stand freely, are each wearing their original woolen costumes of various regimental wear. Four have their original paper labels "Tomac Toys, Bearsden Glascow, Made in Scotland", and the doll are presented in a glass-fronted box with Scottish plaid paper cover. Excellent condition. Mid-20th century. $400/500

92. French Bisque Bébé by Jules Steiner with Beautiful Cafe-au-Lait Complexion

18" (46 cm.) Bisque socket head with light brown complexion (so-called "cafe-au-lait" or mulatto), brown glass inset eyes, dark painted lashes, thickly-fringed brows with feathered details, accented nostrils and eye corners, slightly-parted lips with a double row of tiny teeth, pierced ears, black mohair fleecy hair over Steiner pate, Steiner brown composition fully-jointed body, antique costume included. Condition: generally excellent. Marks: J. Steiner Bte SGDG Paris Fre A 11 (head) (original Steiner paper label on body). Comments: Jules Steiner, circa 1889. Value Points: rare features include luminous golden-tawny complexion with flawless color, original wig, pate, body and body finish, rare double row of teeth. $3000/4000

93. Pretty French Bisque Bébé with Cafe-au-lait Complexion

13" (33 cm.) Bisque socket head with amber brown complexion (so-called "cafe-au-lair' or mulatto), large amber brown glass paperweight inset eyes, dark eyeliner, lushly-painted dark lashes, brush-stroked black brows, accented eye corners and nostrils, slightly-parted lips, row of teeth, pierced ears, black fleecy hair over cork pate, French brown composition and wooden fully-jointed body, antique dress, undergarments, bonnet, socks, and shoes. Condition: generally excellent. Marks: 4. Comments: Emile Jumeau, circa 1895, the doll is shown in the book, *The Beautiful Jumeau* by Florence Theriault. Value Points: very beautiful flawless complexion enhanced by dramatic eyes, original body and body finish. $2500/3500

94. French Bisque Automaton Known as The Russian Tea Server by Lambert

20" (51 cm.) Standing upon a velvet-covered base is a bisque-head doll with large amber brown glass paperweight inset eyes, dark eyeliner, painted lush lashes, brush-stroked and multi-feathered brows, accented nostrils, closed mouth with shaded lips, pierced ears, blonde mohair wig over cork pate, French carton torso and legs, wire upper arms, bisque forearms. Condition: generally excellent. Marks: Depose Tete Jumeau Bte SGDG 4 (head) (remnants of original paper tune label on under-base). Comments: Leopold Lambert, circa 1892, with commissioned head from Jumeau; when wound the doll turns her head from side to side, nods, and alternately moves the tray and tea pot as though pouring tea; the model was

marketed as the Russian Tea Server. Value Points: the doll wears her factory-original silk costume with silk and metallic fringe trim, pearl ornaments, elaborate headdress, and carries wooden tea tray and tea pot. $5000/7500

95. Very Beautiful French Bisque Bébé Steiner with Cafe-au-Lait Complexion

23" (58 cm.) Bisque socket head with amber-brown complexion known as "cafe-aut-lait" or mulatto, very large amber-green glass paperweight inset eyes, thick dark eyeliner, painted black lashes and brows with feathered detail, accented eye corners and nostrils, open mouth with slightly-parted lips, row of tiny porcelain teeth, pierced ears, black fleecy hair over Steiner pate, Steiner brown composition fully-jointed body, wearing antique muslin and silk island dress with silk shawl, plaid silk turban, earrings, undergarments, tacked-on silk slippers. Condition: generally excellent. Marks: A -15 Paris Le Parisien Bte SGDG A-15 (head) Le Petit Parisien Bébé Steiner Medaille d'Or Paris 1889 (body). Comments: Jules Steiner, circa 1890. Value Points: superb flawless bisque with beautiful complexion enhanced by dramatic eyes and eye decoration, original body and body finish, antique costume that is likely original. $3500/4500

rare inserted sideburns and moustache, original body and wearing wonderful original court costume with embroidered detail on purple silk jacket cuffs and vest. $1100/1500

97. Exquisite Early English Poured Wax Lady Doll with Original Costume

18" (46 cm.) Poured wax shoulder head of adult lady with oval slender face and elongated throat, narrow blue glass enamel inset eyes with outlined eye sockets, closed mouth with tinted lips and cheeks, light brown wig of tightly-plaited double coronet captured under a cap of aqua silk looped ribbons, muslin softly-stuffed body with poured wax lower arms and legs in slender elongated shape, dainty bare feet. Condition: generally excellent, some typical paint fading of facial features. Comments: probably English, early to mid-19th century portrait-like doll with exquisite coiffure, wearing original frail silk gown with lace and ribbon trim, matching leggings, undergarments. $1800/2200

98. Charming German Wax-over-Paper Mache Taufling Baby

9" (23 cm.) Wax-over-paper-mache head with solid dome and flat-cut neck socket that attaches to torso neck dowel, almond-shaped brown glass enamel inset eyes, tinted brows, accented nostrils and eye corners, closed mouth, paper mache shoulder plate, lower torso, hands and feet, wooden lower arms and legs, twill upper arms and legs, and twill midriff enclosing crier bellows. Condition: generally excellent, twill slightly dusty. Comments: Sonneberg, circa 1860, the historically-important doll model was influenced by the Japanese Ichimatsu doll introduced to French and German doll makers at the mid-19th century international fairs, and became the predecessor to the articulated child doll (bébé). Value Points: wonderful petite size of the well-preserved early doll. $800/1200

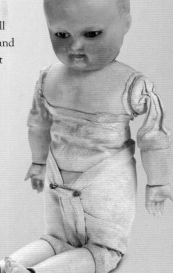

96. Rare Early Wax Courtly Gentleman with Sideburns and Moustache

17" (43 cm.) Poured wax shoulder head of adult man with slender face and throat, high forehead and aquiline nose, blue glass enamel eyes, closed mouth, sculpted ears, inserted hair wig that is waved from her face, inserted brows, moustache and sideburns, slender muslin body with stiffened canvas lower legs and arms, separated fingers. Condition: very good, touch-up to nose tip, hair a bit sparse at forehead, some fraility to ivory satin of costume. Comments: early 19th century. Value Points:

99. Fine Large Grodnertal Wooden Lady with Swivel Waist and Sculpted Comb

25" (64 cm.) All-wooden doll with finely-carved facial features, hair and body, featuring short black sculpted hair with deeply-defined curls surmounted by a decorative comb with gold decorations and having fine stippling detail of hair around the forehead, elongated throat, sculpted ears, painted brown eyes, beautifully-shaped nose, closed mouth, sculpted detail of gown-bodice edge, all-wooden body with adult lady shape, swivel-waist, dowel-jointing at shoulders, elbows, hips and knees, painted cream lower arms and legs, orange shoes, wearing 1830-era style costume of vintage fabrics. Condition: structurally excellent, the painting is so pristine as to indicate long-ago restoration although none is indicated through black light analysis. Comments: Grodnertal, Empire period, circa 1810. Value points: exceptionally beautiful face with regal presence, rare detail of sculpted hair, large size, and rare waist swivel. Ex-collection of Madeline Merrill, noted doll researcher and author of *The Art of Dolls*, 1700-1940. $7000/11,000

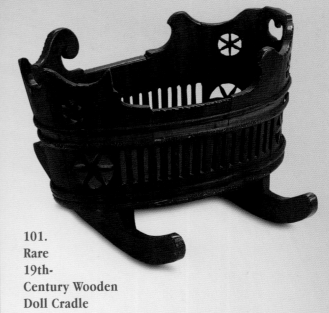

101.
Rare
19th-
Century Wooden
Doll Cradle

13" (33 cm.) The oval-shaped wooden cradle is constructed in a barrel-like fashion with separately-formed panels that are securely-attached by bentwood strips, with vertical slats at the sides for ventilation and vision as well as decorative; other decorations include classic wheel or star-shaped cut-outs and elaborate scrolls or rounded edges. Excellent condition, original finish, one scroll tip missing. Scandinavian, mid-19th century, a rare small doll size of the classic cradle of this region. $400/600

102. An All-Original Early German Paper Mache Doll with Superb Costume

13" (33 cm.) Solid domed head of paper mache or wood pulp with painted complexion over gesso, flat-cut neck socket that attaches to protruding dowel in torso neck, blue glass inset eyes, painted brows, accented

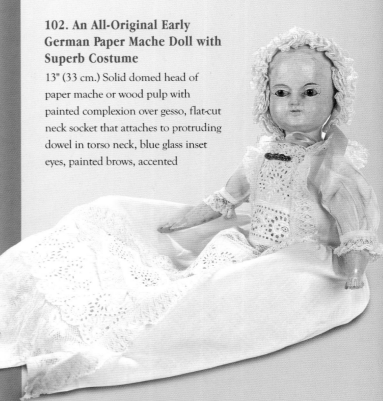

100. Grand French Bisque Poupée by Barrois with E.B. Signature

27" (69 cm.) Pale bisque shoulder head with plump facial modeling, very full cheeks, pale bisque with subtle blushing on cheeks, eyelids and chin, almond-shaped cobalt blue enamel eyes, dark eyeliner, painted lashes and brows, accented nostrils, closed mouth with outlined lips, unpierced ears, new brunette mohair wig over cork pate, French kid gusset-jointed body with stitched and separated fingers, wearing blue silk gown in the antique style, undergarments, antique leather boots. Condition: generally excellent, body is French poupée albeit not original to the doll. Marks: E. B. dep. (front shoulder plate) Jumeau Medaille d'Or Paris (body). Comments: Barrois, circa 1865. Value Points: striking large poupée with brilliant cobalt eyes, very beautiful complexion and painting. $2800/3500

103.

103. German Bisque Lady Doll with Cobalt Blue Glass Eyes

14" (36 cm.) Pale bisque swivel head on kid-edged bisque shoulder plate, elongated slender face and throat, small cobalt-blue glass inset eyes, painted all-around lashes, incised upper eyeliner, feathered brows, accented nostrils and eye corners, closed mouth with downcast lips, pierced ears, brunette mohair wig, kid gusset-jointed body. Condition: generally excellent. Marks: 14 (head). Comments: Germany, circa 1870. Value Points: lovely early lady doll has brilliant eyes that contrast the pale complexion, original early fashion dress, undergarments, leather boots, and wonderful early bonnet. $900/1300

104. German Bisque Lady with Sculpted Blonde Hair in Braided Coronet

25" (64 cm.) Bisque shoulder head turned to the side, blonde sculpted hair with neatly-arranged ringlet curls framing the forehead and a loosely-braided coronet at her crown above arranged curls at the back, sculpted pierced ears, painted facial features, blue upper-glancing eyes, red and black eyeliner, single-stroke brows, accented nostrils and eye corners, closed mouth with accent line between the lips, old muslin stitch-jointed body, sewn-on stockings and shoes, leather arms, lovely green silk taffeta gown with black lace and silk fringe trim, cut-work undergarments. Condition: generally excellent. Comments: Germany, circa 1880. Value Points: very beautiful angelic face with rare coiffure, fine sculpting including well-defined eye sockets, choice bisque and painting. $600/900

104.

105. German Bisque Lady Doll with Cobalt Blue Glass Eyes and Sculpted Jewelry

18" (46 cm.) Bisque shoulder head with blonde sculpted hair waved away from the face into rolled curls behind the partially sculpted ears, with gilt-edged black hair band at the crown, blue glass inset eyes, painted lashes, black eyeliner, arched brows, accented nostrils and eye corners, closed mouth, new muslin body and new bisque limbs, nicely costumed. Condition: the back shoulder plate has been broken off in one piece and reglued; there is no overpaint. Comments: Germany, circa 1870. Value Points: exquisite beauty with serene expression, the lady has sculpted gilded earrings and sculpted necklace. $300/400

105.

nostrils, closed mouth, defined double chin, composition torso, all-wooden fully-articulated limbs with loose-ball-joints at hips, knees, shoulders and elbows, bare feet. Condition: generally excellent. Comments: Sonneberg, circa 1870. Value Points: very rare doll with original finish that is wonderfully-preserved, fully-articulated body, and wearing superb original costume with cutwork and embroidery, matching bonnet. $900/1300

108.

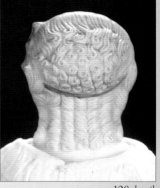

108 detail.

106. German Porcelain Lady Doll with Fancy Blonde Sculpted Hair

20" (51 cm.) Porcelain shoulder head of adult lady with slender face and elongated throat, pale blonde sculpted hair waved away from her face into extended ringlet curls onto her back shoulders and decorated with a black-beaded sculpted clip, painted blue upper-glancing eyes, red and black upper eyeliner, single-stroke brows, accented nostrils, pertly-shaped lips, muslin stitch-jointed body, leather arms, lovely green taffeta antique gown, undergarments, slippers. Condition: generally excellent. Comments: Germany, circa 1870. Value Points: elegant presence is enhanced by rare coiffure, especially lovely sculpting of hair at the back. $400/500

107. Petite German Porcelain Doll with Pale Blonde Sculpted Hair

12" (30 cm.) Porcelain shoulder head with very pale complexion, very light blonde sculpted hair waved away from her face in arranged ringlet curls and captured by a black hair band at her crown, painted bright blue eyes, red and black upper eyeliner, single-stroke brows, accented nostrils, closed mouth with slightly-smiling expression, French kid poupée body with stitched and separated fingers, wearing newer coral silk gown, undergarments. Condition: generally excellent. Comments: Germany, circa 1875. Value Points: well-detailed sculpting of unusually-colored hair. $300/500

108. Petite German Bisque Lady With Long Blonde Ringlet Curls

12" (30 cm.) Pale bisque shoulder head with oval face and elongated throat, pale blonde sculpted hair arranged in horizontal curls that frame her face and edged at the crown with a glazed blue hair band and bow and narrow hair braid; the blue ribbon extends around the back of her hair and separates tightly-arranged curls and seven long ringlet curls that extend onto her shoulders. She has bright blue eyes with black upper eyeliner, accented nostrils and eye corners, closed mouth, sculpted pierced ears, muslin stitch-jointed body and bisque lower limbs, painted black flat shoes, wearing dainty white cotton gown with hand embroidery at the hem, undergarments, earrings. Condition: generallye xcellent. Comments: Germany, circa 18970, Conta & Boehme. Value Points: very rare coiffure with an imagination arrangement of varying curls, braids, ribbons and bows. $900/1300

109. Very Rare German Bisque Lady Doll with Sculpted Bow-Trimmed Green Head Scarf

13" (33 cm.) Bisque shoulder head depicting an adult lady with slender facial shape, sculpted dark-green head scarf that encloses her hair excepting brown sculpted curls at the forehead, the scarf

109.

109 detail.

is decorated with brown edging, and falls onto her shoulders in a cape-like fashion, with sculpted green bows extending down the back, painted small downcast eyes, black and brown upper eyeliner, single-stroke brows, aquiline nose, closed mouth with solemn-shaped lips, defined chin, muslin stitch-jointed body, bisque lower limbs, painted black flat shoes, wearing antique green silk gown. Condition: generally excellent. Comments: Germany, circa 1870. Value Points: very rare model with exquisite detail of facial modeling, rare dark brown hair and sculpted head wrap. $1800/2500

110 detail.

110. German Bisque Lady with Sculpted Brown Hair and Gold Beaded Ribbons

12" (30 cm.) Bisque shoulder head with deeply comb-marked light brown sculpted hair arranged with forehead curly bangs, hair waved back over partially-sculpted pierced ears and arranged in a loosely-coiled chignon at the back with tumbling curls onto her nape; the hair decorated with three bands of beaded gold bands, having large blue painted eyes in deeply-set eye sockets, painted black

111.

upper eyeliner, single-stroke brows, aquiline nose, closed mouth, muslin stitch-jointed body with bisque lower limbs, rose silk gown, and undergarments. Condition: generally excellent. Marks: 10. Comments: Germany, circa 1870. Value Points: rare model with beautifully-shaded and sculpted brown hair and gilded hair ornaments. $900/1300

111. Rare German Bisque Lady with Sculpted Fancy Coiffure and Bodice

20" (51 cm.) Bisque shoulder head of adult lady with slender face and elongated throat, sculpted wheat-blonde hair with an elaborate cluster of curls at her forehead and deeply-looping curls drawn away from her face and decorated with a black bow at her crown and interwoven black ribbons, painted blue eyes, rd and black upper eyeliner, single-stroke brows, accented nostrils and eye corners, closed mouth with center accent line, sculpted Dresden collar ruffle in shaded blue with centered bow, pierced ears, old muslin body with carved wooden lower arms and legs, painted boots, lovely gown in the antique style and undergarments. Condition: generally excellent. Marks: (old pencil script "ib/uo" on inside shoulder plate). Comments; Germany, circa 1870. Value Points: rare hair color and coiffure, elaborate Dresden collar. $1200/1500

112.

113. German Brown-Complexioned Baby with Rare Pigtails by Marseille

8" (20 cm.) Solid domed bisque head with rich brown complexion, tinted black baby hair with three original holes for insertion of mohair black curly pigtails tied with red silk ribbons, brown glass sleep eyes, black painted lashes and brows, open mouth with two tiny lower teeth, brown composition baby body, cotton print romper suit. Condition: generally excellent. Marks: AM Germany 351 14/0 K. Comments: Marseille, circa 1925, included with the doll is a 1974 hand-written note from doll historian, Dorothy Coleman, indicating "I have never seen any with these pigtails before". Value Points: rare and delightful variation of hair style on the rarer brown-complexioned baby marketed as "My Dream Baby". $700/1000

114. Rare German Brown-Complexion Bisque Child, 949 by Simon and Halbig for the French Market

114.

18" (46 cm.) Bisque socket head with light-brown complexion, long-cheeked modeling, large amber-brown glass inset eyes, black eyeliner, thick black painted lashes, black brush-stroked and feathered brows, accented nostrils, open mouth, four porcelain teeth, brown composition and wooden ball-jointed body, new silk and velvet costume included. Condition: generally excellent. Marks: S 11 H 949 (head) Aux Enfants Sages...Paris (paper label on body). Comments: Simon and Halbig circa 1885, the doll was commissioned by the luxury Parisian doll shop Aux Enfants Sages. Value Points: pristine condition with flawless bisque, deeply-sculpted features, original body and body finish, original doll shop paper label. $2000/2800

112. Large German Brown-Complexioned Character Baby by Marseille

23" (58 cm.) Solid domed bisque head with flanged neck, rich brown complexion, black tinted baby hair and brows, small brown glass sleep eyes, accented nostrils and eye corners, closed mouth with coral-shaded lips, firmly-stuffed muslin baby torso, disc-jointed arms and legs, muslin upper thighs, nicely costumed. Condition: generally excellent. Marks: AM Germany. Comments: Marseille, circa 1925. Value Points: rare large size, beautiful glowing complexion, rare and original body style. $500/700

115. German Bisque Portrait of Asian Child, 1329, by Simon and Halbig

17" (43 cm.) Amber-tinted bisque socket head, brown glass sleep eyes, black painted brows with feathering detail, painted black lashes, accented nostrils and eye corners, open mouth, four porcelain teeth, pierced ears, black mohair wig, amber-tinted composition and wooden ball-jointed body, charming newer costume of blue brocade silk. Condition: generally excellent. Marks: Simon & Halbig 1329 Germany

113.